At the Sea

Floor Café
Odd Ocean Critter Poems

Written by **Leslie Bulion**

Illustrated by **Leslie Evans**

PEACHTREE
ATLANTA

For my dive buddies, Corinne and Jerry,
and for my lifelong dive buddy, Rubin
—*L. B.*

To Laurie McHargue: friend, seaside explorer,
and fearless animal rights crusader since we were kids
—*L. E.*

Published by
PEACHTREE PUBLISHERS
1700 Chattahoochee Avenue
Atlanta, Georgia 30318-2112
www.peachtree-online.com

Text © 2011 by Leslie Bulion
Illustrations © 2011 by Leslie Evans

Book design by Leslie Evans and Loraine M. Joyner
Typesetting by Melanie McMahon Ives

Artwork is from original hand-colored linoleum block prints on 100% rag archival paper and digital. Text is typeset in International Typeface Corporation's Slimbach by Robert Slimbach and ITC's Stone Sans by Sumner Stone and John Renner; title is typeset in Parma Petit Normal by Manfred Klein.

Printed in November 2010 by Tien Wah Press in Singapore
10 9 8 7 6 5 4 3 2 1
First Edition

Library of Congress Cataloging-in-Publication Data

Bulion, Leslie, 1958-
  At the sea floor café: odd ocean critter poems / written by Leslie Bulion ; illustrated by Leslie Evans.
    p. cm.
  ISBN 978-1-56145-565-2 / 1-56145-565-2
  1. Marine animals--Juvenile poetry. 2. Children's poetry, American. 3. Humorous poetry, American. 4. Marine sciences--Juvenile literature. I. Evans, Leslie, 1953- ill. II. Title.
  PS3602.U386A85 2011
  811'.6--dc22

                                        2010026691

Contents

Dive In!

Let's visit a habitat shallow and deep,
and boiling hot, where acids seep,
and frigid and pressured and mountainy-steep,
Come explore the sea!

Examine odd critters, enormous and tiny,
sunlit reef toasty and arctic ice briny,
jelly-ish, delicate, venomy, spiny.
They all live in the sea.

They're hunters and foragers, hiders and peekers,
continuous feeders and one-meal-a-weekers,
they're swarmers, attachers, attackers, and sneak-ers.
They all thrive in the sea.

They drift in the currents, they're darting, they're bolting,
they're eelish, concealish, electrically jolting,
they're brightly-hued, luminous, slightly revolting.
Come see them in the sea.

The ocean is planet Earth's main attraction,
Yet humans have fathomed the tiniest fraction.
Now we go deeper into the action—
Dive in and see the sea!

Party Poppers

Bubbledee troubledee,
Sponge-dwelling social shrimp
Clack one big claw to make
Trespassers stop.

Causing explosions
Crustaceanologically,
Filling the ocean with
Snap crackle POP!

Snapping shrimp are small warm-water shrimp that can clack their bigger front claw so fast that it shoots out a jet of water, forming an underwater bubble. The bubble collapses with a *snap!* Predators that come too close can be injured by shock waves. Prey, such as marine worms and small fish, can be stunned or even killed.

When an intruder nears the shrimp colony, one shrimp snaps a warning: *back off*. Soon, others pick up the signal and join in the snapping to chase the intruder away.

Walk Like a Nut

This octopus walks backward on two arms,
And wraps the other six around its top.
It ambles free of predatory harms,
And thus avoids becoming shark-chewed slop.

It winds six tentacles around its top,
Pretending to be flotsam sharks ignore,
And treads away from trouble, flippy flop,
Instead of being chomped to guts and gore—

A coconut that strolls across the ocean floor.

The **coconut octopus** wraps six of its arms around its head and walks backward on its other two arms. This movement makes the octopus look like a coconut drifting across the shallow sea floor near Indonesia. Predators hunting for an eight-tentacled snack pass on by.

The Leopard Sea Cucumber and the Emperor Shrimp

I inch along.

We hitch a ride.
We tour the seafloor countryside.

I'm ship.

We're crew.
We swab the decks
By eating scummy algae specks.

I'm camouflaged
In leopard spots.

While not the swiftest
Of the yachts,
A top-notch spot to meet a mate.

When threatened
I eviscerate.

To spew my guts
Is quite a chore,
And it takes weeks
To grow some more.
But I keep predators away.

We live to crew
Another day.

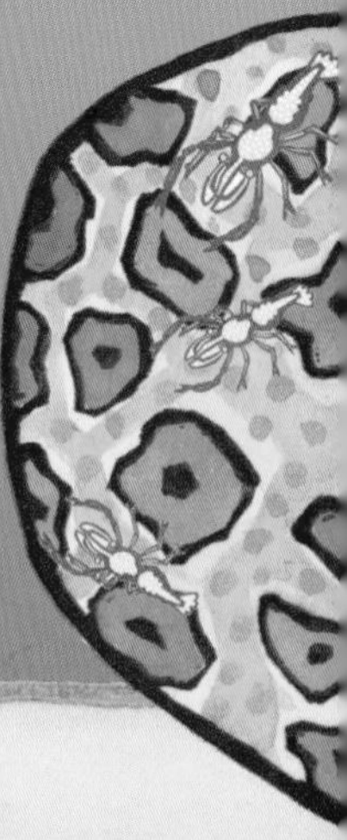

Sea cucumbers are best known for spewing long, sticky, toxic tubules from their insides when disturbed. Some can shoot out many other body organs, too. This is called evisceration.

If a sea cucumber spews toxic guts at a predator, the hitchhiking **emperor shrimp** are also protected. To earn their keep, these small shrimp clean bacteria and algae from the **leopard sea cucumber**'s skin.

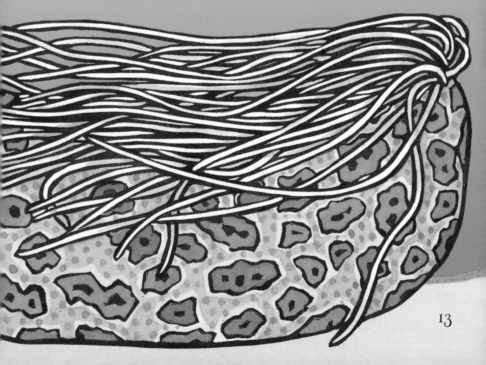

Fish Food

We don't know why the convict fish
Lives so completely hermitish,
Skulks hiding, never swims about,
But eats its young then spits them out.

The little fry in their cave beds,
On mucus strings hung by their heads,
Sleep right above the grown-up's snout,
That eats its young then spits them out.

By day the babes blast from their lair,
A swarming, stripy feeding tear.
They leave the parent home to pout,
That eats its young then spits them out.

When day is done those fry return
(So weird how some kids just won't learn),
Since little convicts, bellies stout,
Get eaten young, then spitten out.

What food can parent convicts prize
When lurking home like ghoulish spies?
Meals babies eat and then respout?
Why eat your young then spit them out?

The convict fish burrows in the coral reefs and rocky bottoms of the warm, southern Pacific Ocean. Adult convict fish stay hidden in their burrows day and night.

Young fish, also called fry, swarm far from their cave each morning in search of food. They find their way back to their caves every evening—quite a feat! Once the fry return, the parent fish takes bunches of them into its mouth then spits them out again, alive. The young convict fish attach themselves to the ceiling of their burrow by mucus threads for the rest of the night.

If parent convict fish never leave their burrows, then what do they eat? Scientists are studying convict fish to find out.

Healthy Eating

patient reef shark waits
a cleaner wrasse dances in—
what's for breakfast?

The **cleaner wrasse** eats tiny, blood-sucking parasites that cling to the skin, mouths, and gills of larger reef fish, rays, and sharks. Cleaners are busiest in the morning when parasites swarm out of the reefs and hop onto host fish. Large fish line up, open their mouths, and spread their gills so cleaners can dart in and use their pincer-like teeth to pick off the pesky invaders.

The cleaner wrasse does a bobbing "dance" and touches the shark with its fins so the shark will relax for a cleaning—*not* make a quick meal of the cleaner.

Crabby Camouflage

Stalk-eyed
hermit defends
each secondhand shell home
with anemone jewelry.
Stunning!

A jeweled anemone crab is a hermit crab
that protects its soft body by moving into an
empty snail shell. The crab camouflages its
borrowed home by sticking colorful, living
sea anemones on the outside of the shell.
Anemones disguise the shell, and can also
sting (and stun) predators that come too
close to the crab. *Ouch!*

Watch the Toes

Near Papua biodiversity's winning;
Sharks stroll the corals and humans are finning.

Scientists believe that the Bird's Head Seascape near Papua province in Indonesia may be home to more kinds of marine life than anywhere else on our planet. That makes it an area of very high biodiversity. Many new kinds of marine animals have been discovered there, including two species of **epaulette shark**.

"Walking" on two pairs of muscular fins lets this slender, three-foot shark wind its way through coral reefs to hunt for crabs, snails, shrimp, and small fish. When we humans swim over delicate corals instead of stepping on them, we are protecting all of the animals and plants that depend on the reef to survive.

Dolphin Fashion

A bottlenose counseled her daughter:
"Put this sponge on your beak underwater.
You can scare out more fish,
Poke sharp stones as you wish,
And your skin'll stay smooth like it oughter."

Some bottlenose dolphins near Australia wear pieces of marine sponge on their beaks.

Scientists think one mother dolphin invented this trick to protect her soft beak from sharp rocks and poisonous stonefish spines as she foraged for food on the seabed. Then she taught her offspring to use the spongy tool, too.

Dolphin daughters seem to learn the behavior, but not dolphin sons.

Upside Down
and All Around

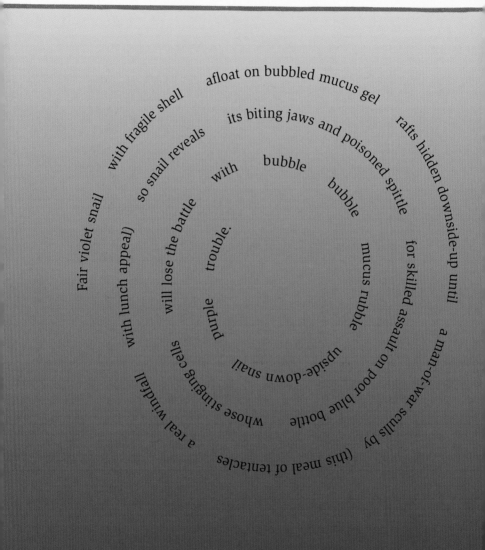

Fair violet snail
with fragile shell
afloat on bubbled mucus gel
rafts hidden downside-up until
a man-of-war sculls by
(this meal of tentacles
a real windfall
with lunch appeal)
so snail reveals
its biting jaws and poisoned spittle
for skilled assault on poor blue bottle
upside-down snail
whose stinging cells
will lose the battle
with
purple
trouble.
bubble
bubble
mucus rubble

The violet snail lives on the surface of tropical and subtropical ocean waters. To stay afloat, it makes a raft of air bubbles surrounded by mucus.

These pretty, quarter-sized snails hang upside down from their bubble rafts and wait to bump into their food— like Portuguese men-of-war, also called blue bottles. Then the snails unfurl strong jaws hidden in a long, snoutlike proboscis and take bites of their prey, paralyzing them with a special purple dye.

Hidden in Plain Sight

Isn't the sea spider strange?
It's mostly all legs and a snout.
And despite its world oceanwide range,
Have *you* ever seen one about?

It's mostly all legs and a snout,
With a body that's twiggy-stick slim.
Have you ever seen one about,
Tiptoeing or having a swim?

With a body that's twiggy-stick slim,
There's no room for guts or for eggs.
Tiptoeing or having a swim,
It sports guts and eggs in its legs.

There's no room for guts or for eggs.
But the snout? Plenty long and quite fierce!
It sports guts and eggs in its legs,
While it prowls for soft sponges to pierce.

The sea spider's snout is quite fierce,
Teeth hidden inside a long straw.
It prowls for soft sponges to pierce,
Then slurps sponge goo up in its craw.

Teeth hidden inside a long straw,
All across its world oceanwide range,
It slurps sponge goo up in its craw—
Now, isn't the sea spider strange?

Sea spiders are not true spiders, but spider cousins who live on the seabed, from the shoreline to the deep-sea floor. They have narrow bodies with little space for internal body parts. Their four to six pairs of legs house digestive organs, eggs, and sperm.

Sea spiders pierce anemones, sponges, corals, and other bottom dwellers with the end of their long, snoutlike proboscis. They use the proboscis to suck up the soft inside parts of their prey.

Dental Health

Reports of narwhals locking horns,
like ancient dueling unicorns,

or sparring rivals, tusk to tusk,
or actions similarly brusque,

appear beside the point because
each spiral tooth from narwhal jaws

contains ten million nerves to sense
environmental evidence,

with messages for narwhal brains,
like Arctic ocean weathervanes.

A cold front looms...where codfish dwell...
a healthy narwhal tooth may tell.

So when we see them crossing spars
and jousting underneath the stars,

one's tusk above and one's beneath,
it's not a fight; they're brushing teeth.

Narwhals are toothed whales with only two teeth. In males, one tooth grows and grows, spiraling six to nine feet into a strong, flexible tusk. Some people think legends of the unicorn came from narwhal sightings.

Narwhal tusks are full of nerve endings that can sense changes in water temperature, pressure, and salinity. When narwhals rub tusks, they may be scraping off coatings of algae and plankton.

Krill Power

thousands
of shrimpy krill
paddle the daytime deep ocean
and hobnob in a beach ball big school
so prowling predators can't recognize
the solid shape of their togetherness
no stragglers to notice at the edges
no single, tasty crustacean
to pick off for
breakfast

and tens
of thousands of these
transparent krill swim and zoom
all goggly-eyed below the sunlit sea surface
in a swarm with a pattern of bodies and spaces
that uses less feathery-legged energy
for swimming and makes finding
the perfect mate
easier

then hundreds of thousands of hungry krill kick at dusk
rising into the surface layer like a flying carpet
youngsters first
then
grown-ups
up
up
up
krill
turbulence
pulling
cold
deep
rich
seawater
up
up
up
a million feathery krill legs churning and stirring
plant food upward into their phytoplankton soup.

Krill are shrimplike crustaceans found in all oceans. Most species of krill are no bigger than your pinky finger, but they swim in huge groups called swarms. Krill swarms are also called schools because krill swim in patterns and formations that help them survive.

Each evening, krill swarm up from deeper water to feed on phytoplankton, the tiny, one-celled plants that grow in the sunlit surface layer. The power of so many krill legs paddling together pulls cold, nutrient-rich water up to the surface. Phytoplankton use the nutrients in seawater for photosynthesis, so by swimming upward, the krill bring fertilizer to their own food crops.

With Her Eggs Tucked Underneath Her Arms

In the vast Atlantic and Pacific,
The common broody squid dives down below.
As caring moms, most squid are not terrific,
But Broody keeps close watch on her squid roe.
In chill and murky seas the whole world wide,
She takes her giant egg sac for a ride.

> With her eggs tucked underneath her arms,
> She swims the inky ocean.
> With her eggs tucked underneath her arms,
> In the depths of devotion.

It's wearying and tiresome to lug that sac all day,
With no time off to grab a bite, and never time to play.
Arms spreading out, then in again—a squid balloon ballet,
With her eggs tucked underneath her arms.

> With her eggs tucked underneath her arms,
> She swims the inky ocean.
> With her eggs tucked underneath her arms,
> In the depths of devotion.

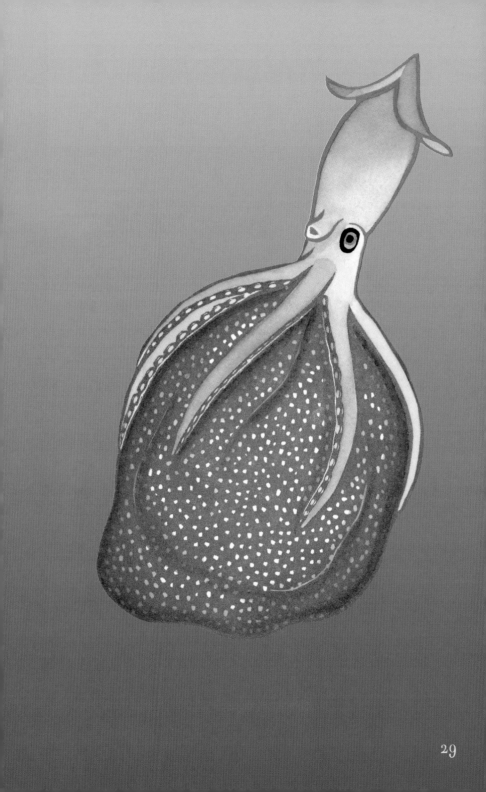

Most other squid will lay their eggs and go,
Though hungry starfish prowl the ocean floor.
They won't fret for an eaten embryo,
Since they have laid so many thousands more.
But Broody's life is dangerous and hard,
Because she keeps each squidlet under guard.

Her egg sac is attached by hooks, which may seem
                                        rather grim.
It billows, then collapses as she takes it for a swim.
And if Broody meets a sperm whale, well, her chances are
                                        quite dim,
With her eggs tucked underneath her arms.

        With her eggs tucked underneath her arms,
        She swims the inky ocean.
        With her eggs tucked underneath her arms,
        In the depths of devotion.

At hatching time, her swimming moves will shake those
                                        eggies out,
And sturdy, strong, new mini-squid emerge and jet about,
With no care for poor Mother who has reached her end,
                                        lights out...
With no eggs tucked underneath her arms.

A **broody squid** swims thousands of feet down into the sea to lay her clutch of two to three thousand eggs. She remains in deep waters for months and cradles her large, billowing egg sac between her arms until the eggs hatch. Most other kinds of squid lay thousands more eggs in clusters on shallower seabeds and die soon afterward.

Swimming with all those eggs uses lots of energy. Deep-diving predators like sperm whales may eat the slow-moving broody squid, but staying on the go ensures that shallow bottom-dwellers like some kinds of starfish and sharks that eat other squids' eggs can't get at her protected sac.

Jellyfishing

Small predatory fishes slink
And hunt throughout the briny drink
For deep-sea prey that hop and sink—
Their favorite wiggly treats.

But up swim stealth siphonophores,
Long jellyrolls with wiggle lures.
Those luminescent matadors
Turn hunters into eats.

Siphonophores (sigh-FON-uh-forz) are colonies of marine animals related to jellyfish. Each part of a siphonophore is a specialized animal, or zooid (ZOH-id), that can't live on its own. A Portuguese man-of-war is a siphonophore with four different kinds of zooids for floating, swimming, eating, and reproducing.

Erenna, a long, transparent deep-sea siphonophore, can make its red, bioluminescent stingers wiggle to look like the movement of tiny crustaceans. Some scientists think small fish swim over expecting a tasty meal, and end up becoming a siphonophore snack instead.

At the Sea Floor Café

For deep-sea seafood we're all set,
We deep-sters eat larvacean slime.
(Great gobs of sinking mucus net.)
For deep-sea seafood we're all set.
Plain boring sea snow's just all wet,
Compared to clogged net past its prime.
For deep-sea seafood we're all set,
Deep sea-sters eat larvacean slime.

Small, soft-bodied **larvaceans** (lahr-VAY-shins) build large mucus houses around themselves to trap food as they float through mid-ocean waters. Every day, larvaceans cast off clogged mucus nets and make new ones.

The old nets snag more tiny animals and food particles as they sink. Sinking larvacean nets provide about half the food needed by deep-sea animals. The rest comes from sinking bits of dead sea plants and animals, called detritus or marine snow, and the dead bodies of larger animals.

The Invasion
of the Bone Eaters

Osedax, the legless worm,
Lands on whale-fall, digs in firm.
Eyeless, mouthless, gills like plumes,
Bone-devouring zombie blooms.

Osedax the gutless wonder,
Egg sac blob and roots down under.
Dines with help of fat bacteria,
At the whalebone cafeteria.

When a larva, or young form, of the
Osedax (OH/seh/dax) worm settles on
the sunken skeleton of a dead whale,
it sends roots deep into the bone.
Microscopic bacteria in the roots help
the worm get the food it needs from
the oils and fats inside the whale bone.

Osedax grows about as long as your
finger. Its feathery gills bloom like flower
petals at the top of its stalk-thin body.
At the stalk's base is a big egg sac,
then below that, the branching roots.

Hooray for the Sea and the ROV

The wide ocean swells across most of our planet.
Our Earth's filled with life; the sea's where we began it.
To explore the seas' wonders we've learned to be clever—
Let's be extra smart and protect them forever.

The **ocean** covers two-thirds of our planet. It is Earth's largest ecosystem, filled with organisms that make a living in wildly different—and even extreme—environments.

So far, humans have only explored about five percent of the global oceans. Advancing technology, including submersibles and remotely operated vehicles (ROVs), allows us to make exciting new discoveries every day. The more we learn, the better we understand how all life on Earth is connected to the health of our oceans.

Glossary

abyssal plain—the flat part of the deep-sea floor

alga—plant or plantlike organism without roots that lives in saltwater or freshwater and uses energy from the sun to make food (two or more are called algae)

bacterium—a one-celled organism that can be free-living or a parasite (two or more are called bacteria)

biodiversity—the different species of animals and plants that live in one area and their interactions

bioluminescent—producing light with chemicals stored inside the organism

brine—water with high concentrations of salt

craw—a pouch in an animal's digestive system to store food that is ready for grinding or chewing

crustacean—a class of invertebrate animal with characteristics that include a hard outer skeleton, a body divided into segments with a pair of limbs on each segment, two pairs of antennae, and a pair of heavy mouthparts called mandibles for chewing and grinding food; most common crustaceans live in water, including shrimp, crabs, and lobsters

detritus—the decomposed remains of dead animals and plants, often broken down into small particles

eviscerate—to cause internal organs to come out of an animal's body

fry—newly hatched or young fish

gills—organs used by animals to take oxygen from water and release carbon dioxide

invertebrate—an animal without a backbone

larva—the newly hatched or young form of an invertebrate, which can look quite different from the adult form (two or more are called larvae)

larvacean—a tadpole-shaped, free-swimming sea animal that builds a giant mucus house around itself to trap and filter food particles

luminescent—producing light at low temperature

marine—found in or having to do with the ocean

marine snow—small particles made up of decomposed remains of minerals and dead animals and plants; the particles sink through the ocean to the sea floor (also called sea snow)

phytoplankton—microscopic one-celled organisms that live in oceans and lakes and can use energy from the sun for photosynthesis; some phytoplankton are more closely related to plants, and some to bacteria

proboscis—a long, flexible mouth-part attached to the head of an animal that can be beaklike or strawlike, and can contain teeth and jaws

remotely operated vehicle—a submarine that can dive deep into the sea for research or work without people aboard, operated by a pilot on a surface ship (often abbreviated as ROV)

roe—the eggs of a fish, amphibian, or invertebrate

school—a group of animals that swim facing in the same direction, spaced in a particular formation

sea snot—an informal name for marine snow

sea vent—a gap in the sea floor where hot fluids seep into the ocean (also called hydrothermal vent)

spar—a long pole, usually on a ship, that supports sails or rigging

swarm—a large group of animals of the same species, often insects, with no definite pattern or organization

tentacle—a long extension from or near the head of a marine animal used for feeding, moving, or sensing

tubule—a small tube

turbulence—movement of water against the normal flow

whale-fall—the carcass of a dead whale that has landed on the sea floor

zooid—a specialized animal that is part of a group and can't live on its own

Poetry Notes

Dive In!

This poem has four groups of lines, called stanzas. Each stanza has four
lines: a set of three lines that rhyme and a refrain that ties each stanza
together. The rhyming lines have four beats:

Let's VI/sit a HA/bi/tat SHA/llow and DEEP

The beat is the part of a word we say more
strongly.
The refrains in this poem have three beats:

COME ex/PLORE the SEA!

Party Poppers

A *double dactyl* poem starts with
a first line made of two nonsense
words. Each nonsense word has the
rhythm STRONG/soft/soft, called
a dactyl. Each line in the poem has
two dactyls:

BU/bble/dee, TROU/ble/dee.

The last line in each stanza has one dactyl and one strong syllable:

PRE/da/tors STOP.

In the second stanza of a double dactyl, the second line is one long word.
In this poem, the first syllable, "cru" of that long, made-up word crustaceanologically (cru-STAY-shin-oh-LAH-jih-klee) should really
belong to the line above it:

CAU/sing ex/PLO/sions cru

STA/cean/o/LO/gi/cally

Walk Like a Nut

The *Spenserian stanza* is a form usually used for serious poetry. Each stanza
has eight lines with five beats, and a ninth line with six beats. The first part
of each beat is soft, and the second part is strong:

a CO/co/NUT that STROLLS a/CROSS the O/cean FLOOR.

Lines one and three rhyme. Lines two, four, five, and seven rhyme.
Lines six, eight, and nine rhyme.

The Leopard Sea Cucumber and the Emperor Shrimp

Two voices are speaking in this poem. One voice is the solitary leopard sea cucumber. The other voice is the chorus of busy emperor shrimp. The rhyme is shared and jumps from voice to voice, using poetry form to echo the animals' relationship and behavior.

Fish Food

A *kyrielle* is a poem that has four-line stanzas that can rhyme in couplets (two rhyming lines in a row) or every other line. The second or fourth line is repeated in every stanza. Sometimes just the last word of the second or fourth line is repeated.

Why EAT your YOUNG then SPIT them OUT?

Healthy Eating

Haiku poetry was first written in Japan more than three hundred years ago. In English, haiku usually have three lines of no more than seventeen syllables all together. Traditional haiku poetry has a strong connection to the natural world. This poem is both a haiku and a riddle. So, what *is* for breakfast?

Crabby Camouflage

The *cinquain* was developed by an American poet who studied ancient Japanese forms like haiku and tanka. A cinquain has five lines. Each line has a specific syllable count: two, four, six, eight, two. The title of a cinquain should also add to the poem's meaning. Many cinquains are written with an image or idea from nature in mind.

Watch the Toes

An *epigram* is a short poem usually written in one or two rhyming couplets. Epigrams are often funny, and may have a surprising twist. The twist in this poem is that sharks and humans are trading their methods of transportation.

Dolphin Fashion

A *limerick* is a five-line poem that is meant to be funny. The first, second, and fifth lines have three beats each and all rhyme. The third and fourth lines rhyme in a couplet, with only two beats in each line.

Upside Down and All Around

Words that have different vowel sounds but end with the same consonant sound, like snail and shell, are called *slant rhyme*. In this poem, the *L* sounds and the run-on sentence (one with no breaks) pull us along the spiral of the snail's shell. Speaking of spirals, this poem is also a *shape poem*.

Hidden in Plain Sight

A *pantoum* stanza is four lines long. The first and third lines rhyme, and the second and fourth lines rhyme. The first and third lines of each next stanza are copies of the second and fourth lines in the stanza just before it. A pantoum can have any number of stanzas. In the last stanza, the second line is a copy of the third line in the first stanza, and the last line of the poem is a copy of the very first line of the poem. Take a look at the repeated lines in the first two stanzas of this poem:

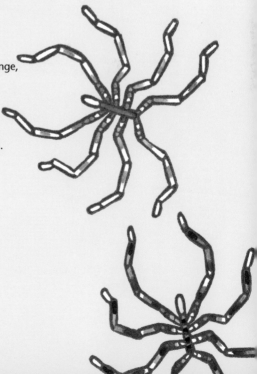

Isn't the sea spider strange?
It's mostly all legs and a snout.
And despite its world oceanwide range,
Have you ever seen one about?

It's mostly all legs and a snout,
With a body that's twiggy-stick slim.
Have you ever seen one about,
Tiptoeing or having a swim?

Dental Health

The couplets in this poem have lines that are four beats long.
The quiet part of the beat is first, and the strong part is second.

It's NOT a FIGHT; they're BRU/shing TEETH.

Krill Power

This poem is *free verse*; it does not rhyme. It is written in one long sentence and is shaped show the continuous changing shape and movement of krill swarms.

With Her Eggs Tucked Underneath Her Arms

When we add melody to a poem it becomes a song, and its words are called *lyrics*. The song's musical notes give the lyrics a specific rhythm. Writing new lyrics to songs we know lets us play with words in a set rhythm. Fun! This poem can be sung to the melody of an old folk song by written by R. P. Weston, Bert Lee, and Robert Harris, called "With Her Head Tucked Underneath Her Arm."

Jellyfishing

This poem has two stanzas with four lines in each. Three of the lines have four beats and rhyme with each other. The fourth lines in every stanza have three beats and rhyme with each other.

At the Sea Floor Café

A *triolet* is an eight-line poem with just two rhyme sounds. Each line has the same number of syllables, or parts of words. The first, fourth, and seventh lines are repeats. The third and fifth lines rhyme with the first line. The second and the eighth lines are repeats, and rhyme with the sixth line. Tricky!

The Invasion of the Bone Eaters

The relentless march of the STRONG/soft STRONG/soft rhythm of each beat in this poem recalls the oncoming invasion of the bone eaters.

Hooray for the Sea and the ROV

These two rhyming couplets have four beats in each line.

Websites to Explore

www.nhm.ac.uk/kids-only/life/life-sea
The website of Britain's Natural History Museum is packed with information about life in the sea, with links to specific information about the ocean, the deep ocean, and many different animal phyla.

www.divediscover.whoi.edu
Dive and Discover is the educational portal of the Woods Hole Oceanographic Institution. It includes information on current expeditions to the sea floor, teacher resources, and a variety of oceanographic and marine biological topics.

www.fi.edu/oceans/oceans.html
The Franklin Institute's Undersea and Oversee web page provides information and links to many excellent oceanographic resources.

www.mbari.org
Monterey Bay Aquarium Research Institute provides a wealth of information about the many exciting investigations of MBARI scientists.

www.montereybayaquarium.org/AquariumLibraryWeb/ui/ glossary/glossarySearch.aspx
Monterey Bay Aquarium Research Institute (MBARI) Glossary of Marine Science Terms

Books You Might Enjoy

OCEAN. Dinwiddie, et al. American Museum of Natural History. (DK 2008)

SMITHSONIAN OCEAN: OUR WATER, OUR WORLD. Cramer, Deborah. (Smithsonian, 2008)

Acknowledgments

The wordplay of these verses would not have been possible without the inspiring scientific inquiries that inform my subjects. I am deeply grateful to marine researchers all over the world who continue to study and protect our planet's last frontier, including Dr. Michael Krutzen and his international colleagues, Dr. Brad Siebel, Dr. Bruce Robison, Dr. Steven Haddock, Dr. Claudia Arango, Dr. Eva Toth, Dr. Martin Nweeia, and Dr. A. S. Grutter.

I would like to give special thanks to Dr. John Dower, Dr. J. Emmett Duffy, Dr. Eugenie Clark, Dr. Robert Vrijenhoek and his technician Shannon Johnson, Dr. Christine Huffard, and Dr. Mark Erdmann for their generous and insightful comments on pertinent selections from the manuscript.

The poem "The Leopard Sea Cucumber and the Emperor Shrimp" was inspired by a photo and caption in the November 2004 *National Geographic* article "Fiji's Rainbow Reefs" by Les Kaufman, photographs by Tim Laman.

I am so very grateful for the encouragement and support of Vicky Holifield, Judy O'Malley, and L. Blair Hewes. I am ever indebted to Judy Thiese, Lorraine Jay, Doe Boyle, Leslie Connor, Mary-Kelley Busch, Nancy Elizabeth Wallace, Nancy Antle, and Kathleen Kudlinski for their endless patience, exuberant singing, and continual eagerness to tuck eggs with me.